PHOTOCOPIABLE E

OF

"DON'T LET SPELLING GET YOU DOWN"

Colour this Book and have Fun!

> ### INSTRUCTIONS
>
> INSTRUCTIONS ON HOW TO USE THIS BOOK - TOGETHER WITH **GAMES** (TO CONSOLIDATE THE WORK BEING LEARNT) CAN BE FOUND AT THE **BACK** OF THIS BOOK.

First published in the United Kingdom in 1992 by Tregear publications
© Copyright Tregear Publications and Angela Tregear Liddicoat 1992

All rights reserved. The Copymasters contained in this publication are protected by international copyright laws. The copyright of all materials in the "Don't Let Spelling Get You Down" Colour this Book and have Fun series, remains the property of the publisher and the author. The publisher hereby grants to the original purchaser the right to make photocopies direct from the printed book for use in the course of teaching only. Otherwise no part of this book may be reproduced in any form, or by any means directly or indirectly without permission in writing from the publisher.

PRINTED BY:-
BIDEPRINT LIMITED, DAGMAR MEWS, KING STREET, SOUTHALL, MIDDLESEX UB2 5PU TEL: 081-571 1617
SETTING AND ARTWORK BY:-
FERRY TYPESETTERS LIMITED, 60 COLDHARBOUR LANE, HAYES, MIDDLESEX UB3 3ES TEL: 081-573 1584

46 Thornhill Road
Ickenham
Middlesex UB10 8SG

FOREWORD

Over the past 15 years I have encountered many adults and children who have found a particular set of words difficult to spell. Despite various methods and the best efforts of pupils, teachers and students, a list of common errors always remained. To combat the problem I have tried out various techniques, including spelling list stories and amusing mnemonics. Mnemonics are systems devised to aid the memory to retain certain information.

This colouring or painting book brings together mnemonics for the most frequently mis-spelt words, enabling <u>all</u> children to tackle spelling with enjoyment, whether or not they have a natural aptitude for it. These methods can be used as a whole class approach and are especially needed by poor spellers now that the National Curriculum puts particular emphasis on correct spelling.

The pace of learning words from this book varies from child to child, but as a general rule, a child with spelling difficulties usually learns one a week. The time taken to colour or paint a page, is sufficient to transfer the idea from the short-term to the long-term memory.

A brief look at the completed work every day, is a pleasant approach to over learning.

This is the first of three books, and in preparation of the series I am greatly indebted to my colleagues, pupils, and their parents who tried out the various methods and reported back on their success, giving me their enthusiastic support and then urging me to go into print and share the ideas.

Here then is the first of 3 books, designed to pave the way to a more enjoyable and successful approach to the teaching <u>and remembering</u> of spellings.

The further titles in the series will be Blue Book 2 "Fun with Homonyms" (beech/beach)(would/wood)(to/too) and Green Book 3 "Spelling Lists Can be Fun".

The theme, then, is to learn with fun, and I sincerely hope that this will be the case!

Angela Liddicoat.

Angela Tregear-Liddicoat

For further information on other books in this series, please turn to last page.

Taskmaster Ltd
Morris Road
Leicester LE2 6BR
Tel: 0116 270 4286
Fax: 0116 270 6992

How to use this book - see page 20

Front cover idea from Claudia Newbegin

Illustrations by Louise K. Richardson

Printed by:-
Bideprint Limited, Dagmar Mews, King Street, Southall, Middx. UB2 5PU
Tel: 081-571 1617

mnemonics
(memory aids)

for

irregularly spelt

basic words

*How to use this book
see page 20*

Short  Vowels   Long

 ăpple (ă)    ācorn (ā)

 ĕgg (ĕ)    ēmu (ē)

 ĭnk (ĭ)    īvy (ī)

 ŏctopus (ŏ)    ōval (ō)

 ŭmbrella (ŭ)   ūniform (ū)

Sally Anne is................

Choose your own word starting with a 'd'.

Monday
Tuesday
Wednesday
Thursday
Friday
Saturday
Sunday
Monday
Tuesday
Wednesday

because if they do they explode!

So... many because they dont want to explode!

I to the **end**
will be your fr**i**end.

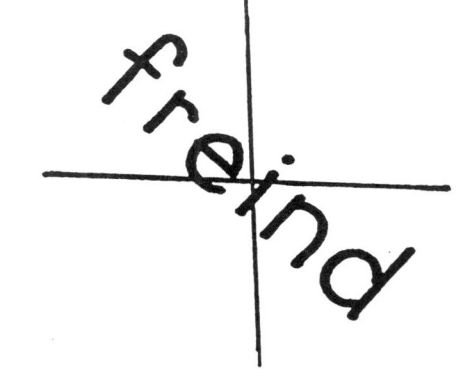

Keep **end** on the
end of fri**end**.

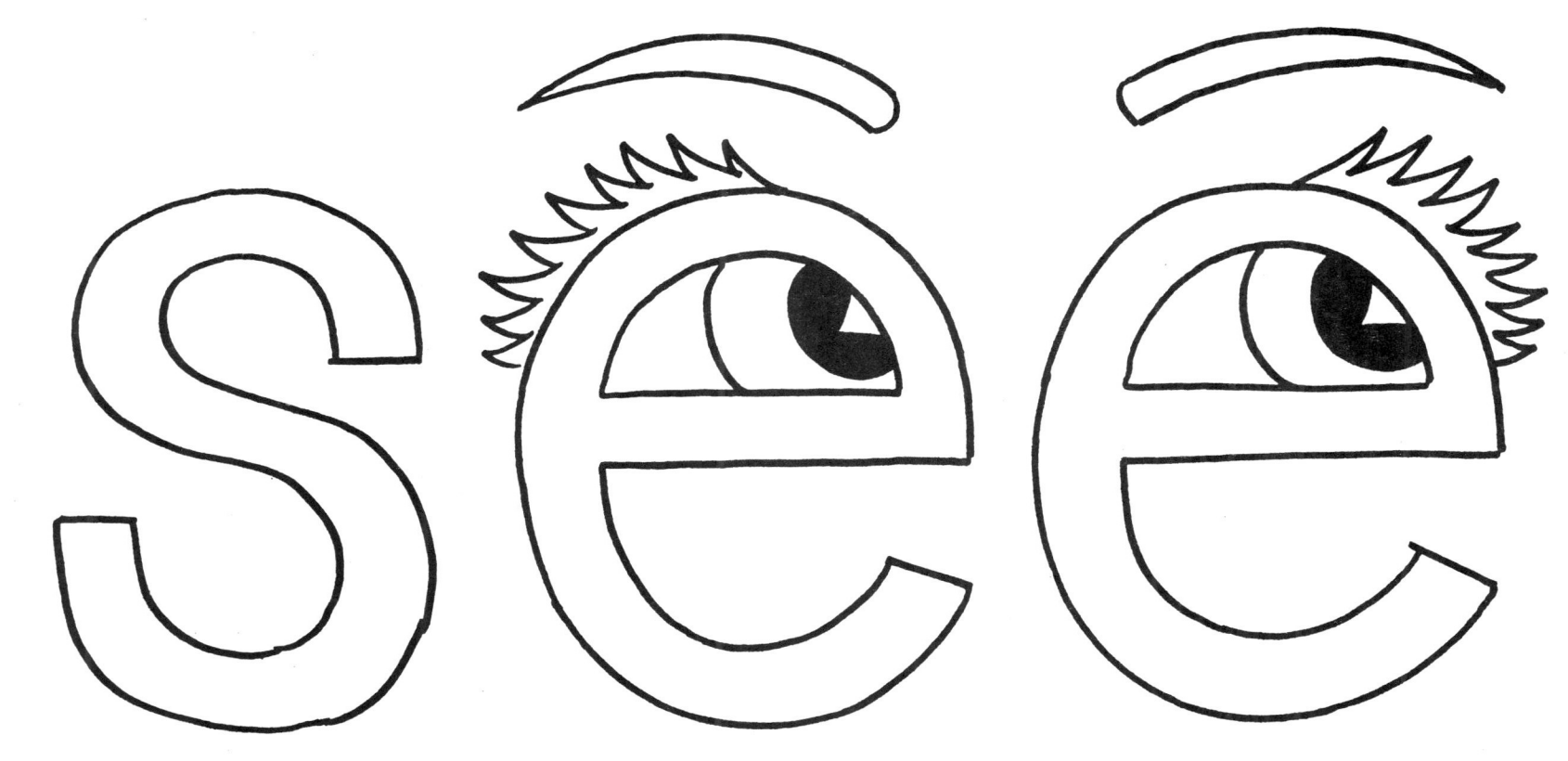

You need 2 eyes
(two)
to see with.

eyes

eyes

Design your own face.

be(birds)c(at)au(rumbs)s(uncle)e(its)(ating)
because

...**because** uncle is a messy eater.

an **island**

is land with sea around it.

island — design this yourself

beaut..... can be beautiful.

(blue/brown eyes, ...nd, ...nusual ...eeth)

add **y** → beauty

add **iful** → beautiful

add **ifully** → beautifully

There is a rat in sep**arat**e.

separate

It is not **necessary** to look old...

never eat hips fat limming salad nd emain oung.

necessary

Write your problem word here, and make up an idea for it.

Look Out for Book 2 and Book 3

How to use this book . . . . . .

Page 2

A mnemonic is a system to aid the memory, and to use this book successfully children must know the NAMES of the letters of the Alphabet, not just the sounds e.g.

(ā) as in apron
(ē) as in emu
(ī) as in ivy
(ō) as in open
(ū) as in uniform

W = double you. Y = Why. U = You etc.

To learn effectively from the other books in the series, which will include spelling family patterns, children should also be familiar with the 'long' and 'short' sounds of the vowels and the 'didactic' marks which indicate them.

Demonstrated the 'didactic' marks (as used in standard dictionaries to indicate pronunciation) by 'clapping' with the child, ie. say apple, say (ă) only one hand clap is possible, therefore describe it as short, say a/corn, say (ā) 2 claps or more are possible, therefore describe it as 'long'. Do the same for egg - (ĕ) 1 clap = short, say emu, say (ē) 2 claps or more - long. Continue with ink (ĭ), (ī) ivy, octopus (ŏ), oval (ō) and umbrella (ŭ), uniform (ū). Colour the page and practise until gradually learnt.

Page 3

SAID sometimes spelt SED/SIAD
Child says: "Sally Ann is ....." and then chooses a word beginning with 'd'. Child then says the chosen sentence, perhaps: "Sally Ann is Dirty.", filling in the chosen word. The child then writes and says S for Sally, (a) for Ann, (i) for is, and 'd' for dirty. If the child spells said SIAD displaying a sequencing problem, he only needs to say "Sally Ann" to get the spelling correct.

Page 4

This picture gives motivation to those children who find sequencing the days of the week especially difficult, because it can only be coloured in when the child has completely mastered the task. The promise of colouring the lion and his friend when the days of the week are recited accurately, encourages the child to put in the extra effort required to overcome their sequencing problems.

Page 5
ANY sometimes spelt ENY
Child says: "Ants never yawn (because if they do they explode)." Then say and write (a) for ants, (en) for never, and (why) for yawn. Then colour and learn.

Page 6
So many MENY. Use same method as previous pages.

Page 7
DOES often spelt DUZ/DOSE
Child says "Daddy often eats sweets', then uses same method. Alternatives are: Daddy often eats sausages or sandwiches. The child then draws the appropriate picture.

Page 8
FRIEND, sometimes spelt FREIND, showing a sequencing problem. Child says: "Keep 'end' on the end of friend." If spelt 'frend' so missing out letter (i) then child says: "I (i) to the end will be your friend."

Page 9
Draw child's attention to the fact that EYE is spelt with its first letter as an (e).

Page 10
Colour in the face to consolidate 'eyes' starting with letter (e).

Page 11
BECAUSE sometimes spelt BECOS
Child says "BECAUSE uncle is a messy eater, the birds eat crumbs as uncle sits eating." Then says and writes (b) for birds, (e) for eat, and so on as before. Then colour.

Page 12
Explain that an island, is land with Sea around it. Then show them the arrow joining the words 'is' and 'land' together making the word ISLAND. (The silent 's' can be thought of as the sea, or a snake.) Then let the child design its own island.

Page 13
To teach children that 'full' as a suffix drops one 'l', but that 'fully' has two 'ls'. The story is used for children too young to understand the rules of suffixing.

Page 14
Beauty, beautiful, beautifully, method as before.

Page 15
ENOUGH sometimes spelt ENUFF.
Child says "Elephants never own ugly great houses." Then says and writes (e) for elephants, (n) for never, and so on as before. Then colour.

Page 16
SEPARATE spelt SEPERATE
Point out that the words 'a rat' are in Sep-a-rat-e. Then colour the page.

Page 17
Necessary, method as before

Page 18
FLUORIDE often spelt FLORIDE.
Ask child to colour in all the letter (u's) in the same colour. Don't miss the one on the tube!

Page 19
Now the techniques are familiar, let the children develop them to overcome their own problem words.

LOOK OUT for Blue Book 2: 'Fun with Homonyms' and Green Book 3: 'Spelling Lists Can be Fun".

Reach the Goal

To Assemble
Photocopy the 'half football pitch twice onto card and then join the two copies along the centre line to form a complete football pitch.

Number of Players
2

Apparatus
One 'Football Pitch' playing board.
1 counter each.
1 Referee needed.
Pencil and paper for each player.

Method of Play
1. Make a list of words which each player is learning and hand it to the referee.
2. Each player places his counter at the start position, and then sits at his goal post.
3. The referee calls out the first spelling and the players write it in on their paper. (Different players may be learning different spellings.)
   If the spelling is correct, the player may move his counter up one section of the field, towards the other player's goal. If their spelling is incorrect, they do not move.
4. The referee then says the next spelling, and players move if correct, or stay where they are if not, (until a player scores a goal and wins - or a draw is declared).
5. Continue playing until all spellings are completed.

*Note:- *Where two players have reached different levels of spelling, simply furnish the referee with those appropriate to each player.*

Reach the Treasure

An alternative board to the football pitch.
Photocopy each half of the "Treasure Island" onto card and then join the two copies along the centre to form a complete island. Play exactly as for the football game:- winner is the one reaching the treasure first.

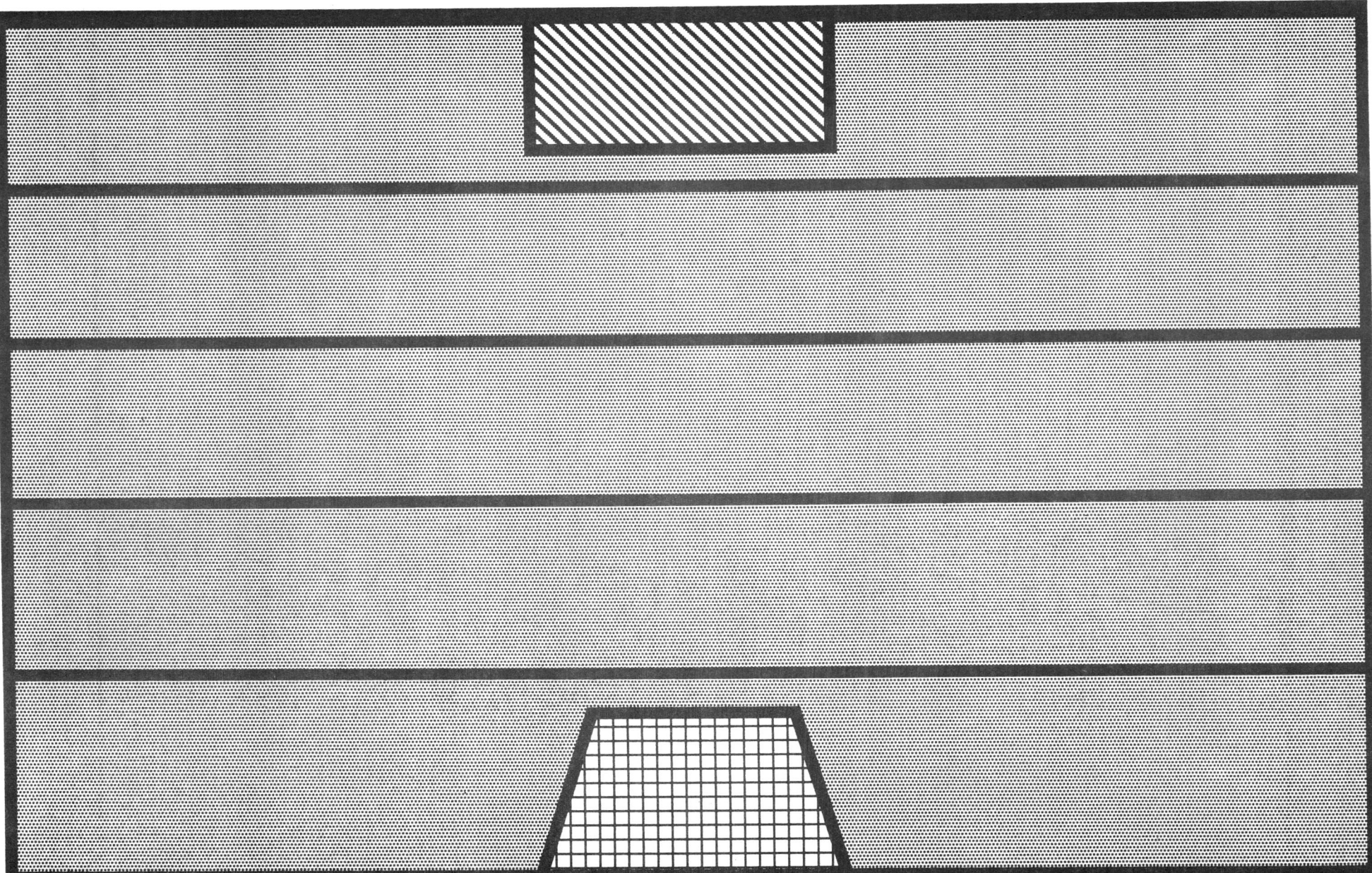

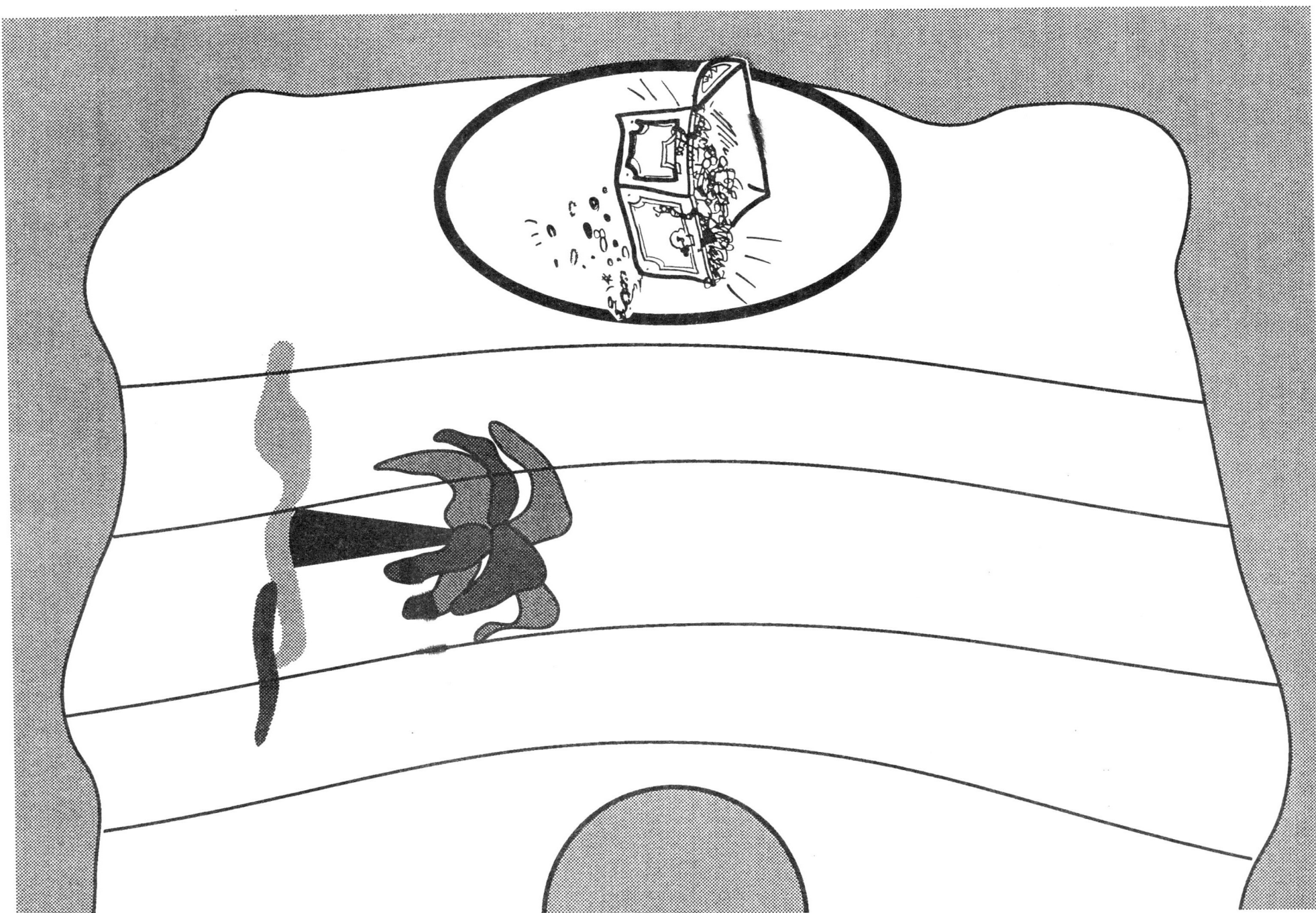

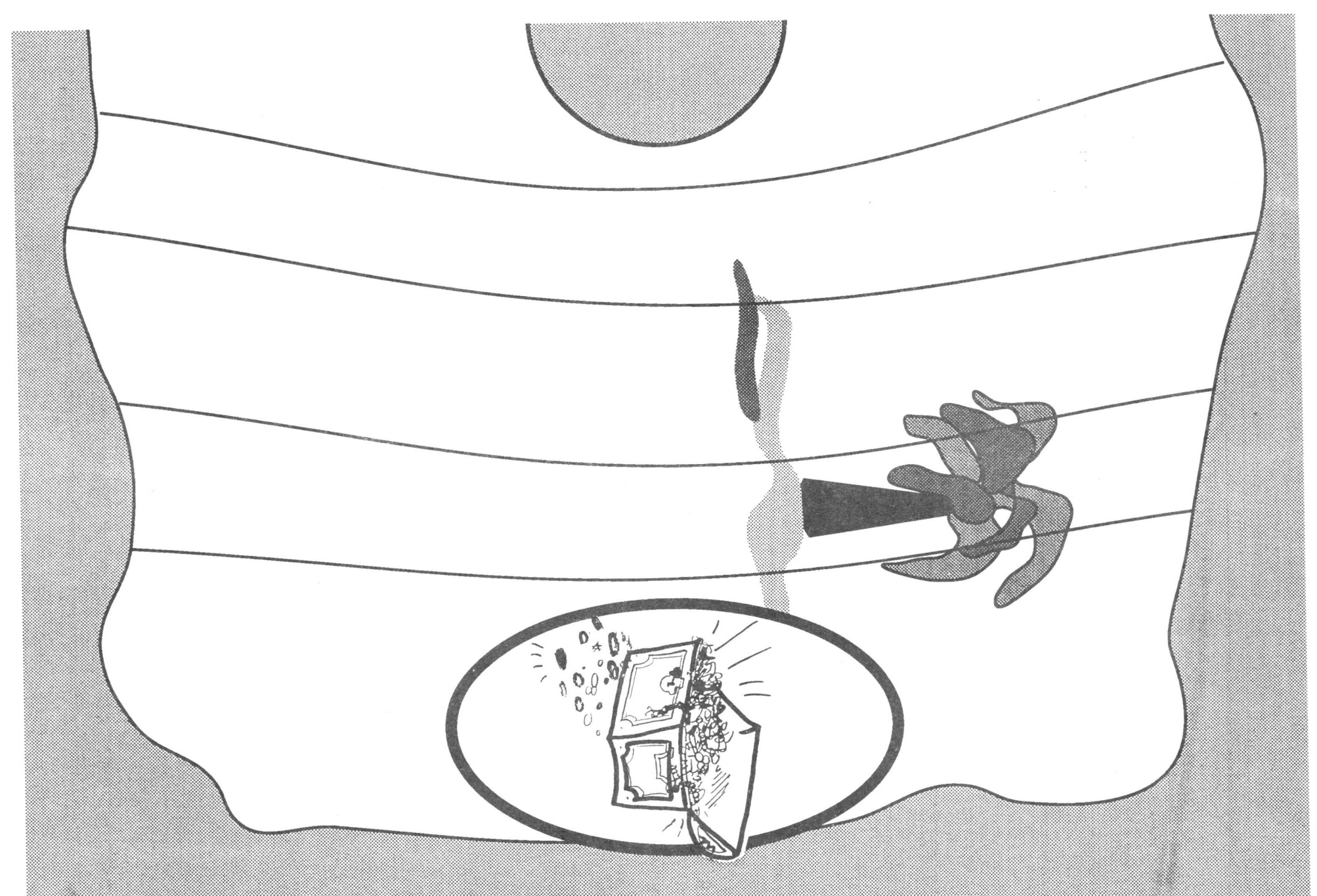